**THE
YOUNG PIANIST'S
LIBRARY
No. 14C**

DENES AGAY

GERSHWIN RECITALS
Best-Loved Songs And Themes
of George Gershwin

Arranged For Piano Solo by DENES AGAY

C O N T E N T S

FASCINATING RHYTHM

Music and Lyrics by
GEORGE GERSHWIN and IRA GERSHWIN

Arranged by Denes Agay

SOMEONE TO WATCH OVER ME

Music and Lyrics by
GEORGE GERSHWIN and IRA GERSHWIN

Arranged by Denes Agay

PRELUDE 2

By
GEORGE GERSHWIN
Arranged by Denes Agay

CONCERTO IN F
(Themes From First Movement)

By
GEORGE GERSHWIN
Arranged by Denes Agay

CONCERTO IN F
(Themes From Second Movement)

By
GEORGE GERSHWIN
Arranged by Denes Agay

Piu mosso

Espressivo con moto

I GOT RHYTHM

Music and Lyrics by
GEORGE GERSHWIN and IRA GERSHWIN

Lively (with abandon)

Arranged by Denes Agay

I GOT RHYTHM
(GERSHWIN IMPROV.)

Music and Lyrics by
GEORGE GERSHWIN and IRA GERSHWIN

Arranged by Denes Agay

Very marked and lively

RHAPSODY IN BLUE

By
GEORGE GERSHWIN
Arranged by Denes Agay

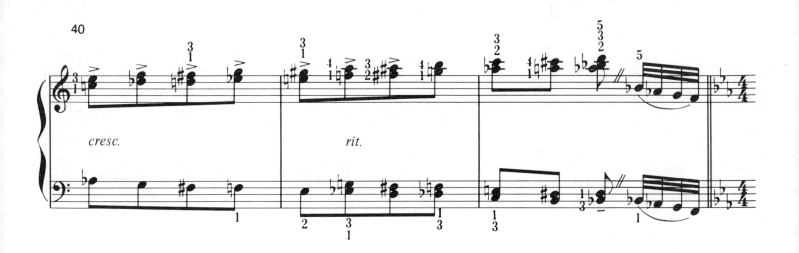

Con moto – Maestoso

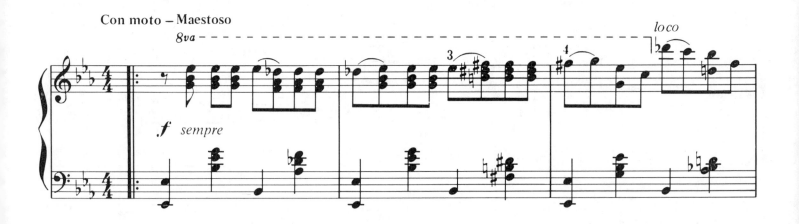

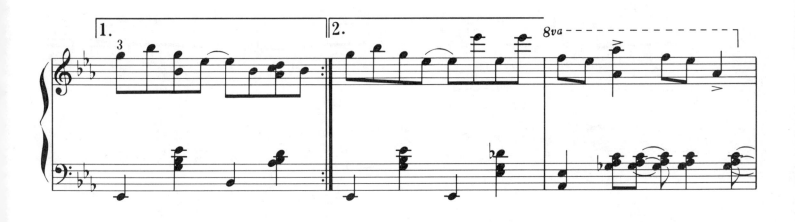